Unlocking the Beauty of

The Catechism

The Creed: Part Two

Facilitator's Guide

Christopher J. Ruff, S.T.L.

Unlocking the Beauty of the Catechism
The Creed: Part Two – Facilitator's Guide

Novo Millennio Press
PO Box 160
La Crescent, MN 55947
www.novomill.com

Nihil obstat: Rev. Jesse D. Burish, S.T.L.
                Censor Librorum

Imprimatur: William Patrick Callahan, OFM Conv.
                Bishop of La Crosse
                January 30, 2013

The *nihil obstat* and *imprimatur* are official declarations that a book or pamphlet is free of doctrinal or moral error. No implication is contained therein that those who have granted the *nihil obstat* and *imprimatur* agree with the contents, opinions, or statements expressed.

Cover art:
Manuel Panselinos, *Christ Enthroned.*
Protaton church, Mount Athos, Greece, ca 1290.
Image compliments of skete.com.

Graphics and Design:
Alice J. Andersen
www.alicejandersen.com.

Introduction

The Facilitator's Role

Welcome to the Facilitator's Guide for *Unlocking the Beauty of the Catechism – The Creed: Part Two* .

Perhaps you are your group's designated facilitator throughout this course of shared study. Or perhaps your group has decided its members will take turns acting as the facilitator, and it is now your turn. Either way, the facilitator's role is a humble but important one.

Let me emphasize one thing right away. You are not expected to have any more wisdom or knowledge about the *Catechism of the Catholic Church* than any other member of the group. The Catechism itself is the teacher, supplemented by the study guide *(Unlocking the Beauty of the Catechism)*. Your primary role, as stated in the study guide itself, is "to start and end the meeting on time, to help keep things moving and on topic, and to foster a friendly, supportive environment in which everyone feels invited to contribute."

The rest of your role can easily be seen in the following excerpt from "Keys to a Successful Catechism Study," taken from the study guide itself.

Conducting the Session

1. The facilitator calls the gathering to order and all pray together the opening prayer.

2. The group participants then take turns reading aloud the study guide material for that session (one or two paragraphs at a time—whatever seems reasonable). This rotating pattern should continue through the discussion questions.

    - **NOTE:** Consistent feedback has confirmed that this practice of reading aloud the study guide material enhances the group experience, even though participants have already read it on their own. Starting with the opening prayer, it typically takes only 10-15 minutes to arrive at the first discussion question.

3. If a discussion question asks for some passages of Scripture to be read, this should also be done aloud if time permits, though it is presumed that people have done this on their own in preparation for the meeting.

4. The facilitator has a Facilitator's Guide with "answer prompts" for some questions, and this may be helpful if the discussion stalls or there is confusion. But the guide should be used sparingly or it will get in the way of genuine discussion. The group should try to answer every question as thoroughly as possible before there is any consultation of the Facilitator's Guide.

5. If in the course of the discussion there arises a question or controversy that cannot be resolved in the group, the facilitator should consult the pastor or another resource person with a solid theological formation between sessions, bringing their response back to the group.

6. When there are 10-15 minutes left in the allotted schedule for the meeting, the facilitator should note that it is time to draw the discussion to a close (even if some discussion questions remain) and to move on to reading the brief "Growth in Discipleship" section, and praying the "Group Prayers of Intercession."

7. The purpose of the "Growth in Discipleship" section is to provide ideas for personal application. These can be discussed if people wish, but there is no need for any commitments to be made publicly, unless people want to plan, for example, to pray the rosary together, or carry out some work of service, etc.

8. The "Group Prayers of Intercession" are intended to be spontaneous prayer intentions. They direct the power of prayer to various needs and simultaneously deepen the spirit of fellowship in the group. Conclude with the Lord's Prayer.

9. The session should end on time, even if members are eager to keep going. This is vital for the health and longevity of the group. The date and place of the next meeting should be confirmed.

10. It is good to follow the meeting with fifteen to twenty minutes of social time for those who are able to stay. Simple refreshments are a nice touch, with emphasis on the word simple. Otherwise people feel pressured to keep up with high expectations.

The Art of Community

Your group is a small community and, like any community, its health and vibrancy will depend on good (though not always perfect!) human relationships. That is the reason the principles of "Group Etiquette" are included on page 18 of the study guide. They should be pointed out at the first session.

Group Etiquette

- Pray for the members of your group between sessions.

- Maintain confidentiality.

- Be a good listener and encourage everyone to contribute to the discussion, without anyone monopolizing. Members that are more talkative should allow everyone a chance to respond to a discussion question before they speak a second time.

- Love your neighbor by speaking charitably and refraining from any kind of gossip.

- Be on time, come prepared, and actively take part in discussion and prayer.

- Be open and expect God's action in your life and prayer—expect to be changed!

The "Answer Prompts"

The remainder of this Facilitator's Guide consists of the discussion questions from the eight sessions of the study guide. Some of them include "answer prompts" in italics. As you know, these are not contained in the study guide itself. They are provided to you as facilitator in the event that they may be helpful, keeping in mind point number 4 in the "Keys" above.

It is natural that group members will want to know, "What does your book say?" And it is fine to tell them, as long as people have made a good effort to give their own answers first.

You will see that many of the discussion questions do not have answer prompts after them. That is the result of a judgment about which ones perhaps needed the extra support, especially for doctrinal clarity, and which ones would be best left to the group members to work through on their own.

May God bless your group's Catechism study and make it fruitful!

Christopher Ruff, S.T.L.

Session 1

Jesus' Suffering and Death

Reflection on
nn. 571-623

We begin Part Two of this study of the Creed with the Catechism's focus on the mysteries of the suffering and death of Christ.

Discussion Questions

1. Have someone read the account of the disciples on the road to Emmaus (Luke 24:13-32). Now have someone (or perhaps 2 people, as it is a bit long) read Isaiah 53, written more than 500 years before Jesus' birth. It must certainly have been one of the Scriptures proclaimed by him that made the disciples' hearts "burn" within them. Imagine yourself listening to Jesus in their place and discuss how you would have felt and reacted.

2. History reveals that Christians have sometimes blamed the Jews for the death of Jesus. What observations of the Catechism in nn. 574-598 are helpful in presenting a more balanced view?

See the Catechism text, as well as the summary from this session. Note particularly from n. 591:

*"Jesus asked the religious authorities of Jerusalem to believe in him because of the Father's works which he accomplished. But such an act of faith must go through a mysterious death to self, for a new 'birth from above' under the influence of divine grace. Such a demand for conversion in the face of **so surprising a fulfillment of the promises** allows one to understand the Sanhedrin's tragic misunderstanding of Jesus..." [emphasis added].*

3. Sometimes we have a tendency to think of sin as simply doing something "against the rules." We feel guilty and hopefully go to Confession. That is better than excusing ourselves, but n. 598 reminds us of the deeper significance of sin.

    - If we look at sin in this deeper way, what changes inside us?
    - What difference does it make when temptation comes along?
    - Is our repentance for sin a different sort of repentance?
    - How would you communicate this deeper understanding of sin to a child? What would you say?

Sin is something intensely personal. Those who sin "crucify the Son of God anew in their hearts (for he is in them) and hold him up to contempt" (n. 598). The knowledge that our sin crucifies Christ who loves us should affect deeply our whole attitude towards it.

4. In n. 612 we read that Jesus felt a natural "horror" at the thought of being put to death. He even prayed that the Father "let this cup pass" if possible.

   Do you think this could be of comfort to people in the face of their own suffering? Discuss.

   *It helps us see the **humanity** of Jesus, so that when we feel pain or fear we know that we are not alone, that he felt it too, that he understands.*

5. The devotional life of the Church offers us a variety
    of ways to pray and meditate on the suffering and
    death of Christ for our salvation (prayerful reading
    of the Passion accounts in the Gospels, the Sor-
    rowful Mysteries of the Rosary, the Stations of the
    Cross, the Divine Mercy Chaplet, etc.). Which of
    these are particularly meaningful to you, and why?

6. Pope John Paul II suffered a great deal from the assassination attempt, from various surgeries, from the humiliating infirmities of old age, and finally from the last stages of the disease that robbed him of his ability to speak (how humbling for the once great orator!) and ended in his death. He often urged the sick and the elderly not to "waste" their suffering.

   • What is at the heart of the difference between wasted suffering and fruitful suffering?
   • Do you think Catholics today are as likely to "offer up" their sufferings as they were a generation or two ago? Why or why not?
   • If you have children (or grandchildren), do you encourage them to offer up their pains and sacrifices?

"Wasted" suffering is pain that is merely resented, complained about, rather than offered to Christ as a share in his suffering for our benefit and the benefit of the world. This does not mean that we should go looking for suffering or fail to try to remedy it. But when inevitable sufferings come our way, we should strive to offer them to God in love. Pope John Paul II had much personal experience of this kind of suffering, together with a special love and esteem for those who are sick, elderly or dying. He saw that they had

a special but hidden gift to offer on behalf of the world. It is the very hiddenness and humility of this gift that makes it so beautiful in God's eyes.

Session 2

From the Tomb to the Right Hand of the Father

Reflection on
nn. 624-682

We continue our study of "Jesus Christ, the Only Son of God," turning to his burial, descent into hell, Resurrection and Ascension to the Father, from whence "he will come again to judge the living and the dead."

Discussion Questions

1. We read in n. 628 that when we are baptized we "die to sin" in order to live a new life. If a life without sin is the fullest, happiest life, then why is renunciation of sin a kind of "death"?

Because of our fallen tendencies inherited through original sin, we are often attracted to what is evil, even though it will ultimately fail to satisfy and end in misery. So the effort to stand strong with God's grace against the seductive power and attractiveness of temptation can feel like a sacrifice, a kind of death. Every day we are called to "die" in some way to our selfishness and pride, our bad temper, lust, laziness, etc. Of course the beauty of that death is that it truly does lead to a resurrection, to a fullness of life and joy that the world cannot give—and that it cannot take away.

2. Read the account of Peter and "the disciple Jesus loved" (probably John) at the empty tomb in John 20:1-10. Notice that while it tells us Peter *saw* the empty cloths, it makes a point to say the "other disciple" saw and *believed.*

   - Contrast the actions of Peter and "the disciple Jesus loved" at the time of Jesus' Passion and death (see Jn 13:12-38; 18:1-27; 19:25-27.)
   - How does this perhaps explain their different reactions at the sight of the empty tomb?
   - What is the lesson for us?

The last time Peter saw Jesus, he denied him three times, while "the disciple Jesus loved" (cf. Jn 13:23) who lay close to Jesus' breast at the Last Supper, stood faithfully beneath the cross as he died, and accepted the gift of Mary as his mother.

Consider, too, the current circumstances: Following Jesus' horrible death, the disciples have hidden out of fear that they may be the next to die. They have taken refuge in the Upper Room, with the doors locked. They probably know that Pilate has posted guards outside Jesus' tomb out of concern that the body might be stolen.

Given these past actions and present circumstances, it is not hard to see why Peter perhaps harbored doubts—or at least did not know what to think—about the empty tomb, while the beloved disciple received a special grace to believe, thanks to his closeness to Jesus and his faithfulness under trial.

The lesson for us is to stay close to Jesus always.

3. The first to encounter the Risen Christ were the women who came to the tomb to anoint his body (Mary Magdalene, etc.), and not the apostles. Is there perhaps a kind of justice here? Discuss.

While all the Apostles except the "disciple Jesus loved" were hiding out of fear, it was the women who showed courage, who stood at the foot of the Cross. Love compelled them to be there, regardless of the danger to themselves. Now, in a stroke of divine justice, Jesus would appear first to these women. How ironic, that in a culture in which women were considered unreliable witnesses in a court of law, Jesus specifically chose women to go and bear witness to the Apostles regarding the greatest event in history, his Resurrection.

4. Some skeptics of the Resurrection of Christ say that the apostles just tricked themselves into believing what they expected so intensely—that Jesus would rise from the dead. What does the Catechism say in nn. 643-644 to show how unreasonable this argument is?

See text. Clearly the Apostles found themselves thrown into confusion and fear at Jesus' death. They were far from expecting his Resurrection, and doubted it even when he actually appeared to them.

5. Through his death and Resurrection, Jesus redeemed us from sin and conquered Satan (though the devil is still permitted to tempt man during his earthly pilgrimage) and death. Possessing such good news, you would think Christians would stand out in the world for their great joy. Yet so often Christians look more or less like everybody else. How do you explain this?

6. With regard to nn. 671 and 672, what are some
    signs that the Holy Spirit is active in the world?
    What are some signs that we are nonetheless living
    in a time of "distress and the trial of evil" (n. 672)?

7. Imagine the Final Judgment (see nn. 678, 679) occurring today. Jesus' loving but serious eye surveys all who have ever lived, measuring human hearts and actions. What is he looking for? What do you hope he would find in you? Before answering, read Mt 25. Then, since no passage of Scripture is meant to be taken in isolation, read also the Sermon on the Mount in chapters 5-7 of Matthew. Put these together to identify the main characteristics Jesus wants to see in a disciple.

The Holy Spirit, Lord and Giver of Life

Reflection on
nn. 683-747

Our focus now turns to the statement of the Creed: "I believe in the Holy Spirit." We reflect on the Spirit in relation to the life of the Trinity and in regard to the story of salvation, from creation to the end of the world.

Discussion Questions

1. The late Cardinal Mercier of Belgium loved to pray daily a short prayer to the Holy Spirit. He told others that if they took just five minutes a day to quiet themselves and to pray this prayer, their lives would be transformed:

    Oh Holy Spirit, Beloved of my soul, I adore You. Enlighten, guide me, console me. Tell me what I must do, give me Your orders. I promise to subject myself to all that You desire of me and to accept all that You permit to happen to me. Let me only know Your adorable will.

    Read this together slowly as you begin your discussion. What do you think of Cardinal Mercier's claim that just five minutes a day with this prayer can transform your life? Discuss.

2. The Catechism quotes St. Paul's phrase that "God has sent the Spirit of his Son into our hearts, crying, *'Abba!'* Father!'" (Gal. 4:6) and it states that "those who believe in Christ know the Spirit because he dwells within them" (687). Have you given much thought to the Holy Spirit? Do you have much of a "feel" for him? What helps you or hinders you in developing a sense of relationship to the Holy Spirit?

3. One of the mysteries of the Trinity is that the Holy Spirit is, **in his very Person,** Love—the Love of the Father and the Son for one another. If that is the case, then what would you expect would be a major fruit of the Holy Spirit in our hearts? Discuss where and how this has been exemplified in human history, giving examples as you are able.

One would expect the Holy Spirit to increase our capacity to love by making us sharers in God's own love ("Come Holy Spirit, fill the hearts of your faithful, and kindle in them the fire of your love…."). In human history this is exemplified in the saints, in their passionate, holy love for God and for neighbor. Think, in our day, of Blessed Mother Teresa of Calcutta. Someone once said to her, "Mother, I wouldn't do the work you do for a million dollars." Her response: "Neither would I." Anyone who reads the lives of the saints will be struck by the fire of love in their hearts that propelled them to holiness.

4. Jesus speaks of the Holy Spirit both as a "Consoler" (John 14:6) and as one who "convinces the world of sin" (John 11:8). This sounds contradictory. How can we explain it?

There is the old saying that God "comforts the afflicted and afflicts the comfortable." That, in some sense, is part of the Holy Spirit's mission. He often touches us with his spirit of loving consolation, especially in the midst of our crosses; on the other hand, he also pricks our consciences with a healthy awareness of our need to repent and be converted when we have sinned (he "convinces us of sin"). After repentance, he is often there again with his consolation.

5. Recall that in Jn 16:13, Jesus calls the Holy Spirit the "Spirit of truth." Who logically stands in direct opposition to this (see Jn 8:44)? How is this battle playing out in the world today?

6. Which of the symbols of the Holy Spirit listed in nn. 694-701 do you find most striking or meaningful (you may list more than one)? Why?

7. The *Catechism* notes in n. 709 that after King David, Israel "gave in to the temptation of becoming a kingdom like other nations."But the Kingdom promised by God would belong only to the "poor according to the Spirit" (n. 709). So Israel had to be purified by the experience of being conquered by Babylon, with her people sent into exile. Humbled, then, a Remnant of Israel was ready to return to being "little" or "poor" before the Lord.

   Where do we see that the Apostles needed to learn similar lessons? How is this paralleled in our own lives?

   The Apostles argued with each other about who was the greatest and were ambitious to sit at the right and left hand of Christ in his kingdom (see Matthew 20:20-27 and Mark 9:33-37). Jesus taught them that they must make themselves little and be of service. See also the washing of the feet in John 13:1-15.

8. The Catechism tells us that in the Old Testament there arose two lines of prophecy, one promising the Messiah, and the other promising an outpouring of the Spirit. As a sampling of this second set of prophecies, have someone read Ezekiel 36:25-28, Jeremiah 31:31-34, and Joel 2:28-32. Then read from Peter's speech on Pentecost showing the fulfillment of these prophecies, Acts 2:17-21.What stands out for you from these passages? Discuss.

9. In Paul's Letter to the Galatians, he writes: "The
    fruit of the Spirit is love, joy, peace, patience, kind-
    ness, generosity, faithfulness, gentleness, self-
    control" (5:22-23). How do you think we can better
    dispose ourselves to receive this beautiful fruit and
    the Holy Spirit who brings it?

I Believe in the Holy Catholic Church

Reflection on
nn. 748-810

We begin to reflect on the statement of the Creed that professes our belief in the Church.

Discussion Questions

1. Why do you suppose Scripture furnishes us with so
    many symbols or images of the Church (sheepfold,
    cultivated field, People of God, building/temple of
    the Holy Spirit, Body of Christ, Bride of Christ)?
    Which is most striking or meaningful to you? Why?

*The Church is such a mystery that one symbol or
image alone can't do justice to it. Each image sheds
light on a particular dimension. It is like exploring
the many facets of a diamond.*

2. Why do you think Christ gave the Church a hierarchical structure constituted by "the Twelve with Peter as their head" (n. 765)? Why not just a "Bible Church" constituted by an assembly of believers in which each depends on direct, personal guidance from the Spirit and nobody has authority over anybody else?

Of course Christ could have set up the Church any way he wished. The fact is that he established a hierarchical structure. Given fallen human nature, that doesn't seem too surprising. Without some sort of centralized authority, every institution seems to come apart, to fragment. That has certainly happened to the Protestant churches, which have fragmented into literally thousands of denominations, each professing its own particular views.

3. Have someone read the two quotes in small print in
    n. 771. Discuss this paradox and the difficulty that
    the secular world has in grasping it.

*The secular world sees only the human dimension
and thus tends to evaluate everything in social/
political terms. It is only by seeing both the human
and the divine dimensions that we can embrace the
Church as the Body of Christ even when her members commit sin. Recall that even Jesus' hand-picked
Apostles included one, Judas, who turned out to be
a traitor. So we are called to persist in faith in the
Church as the Bride of Christ, in spite of the betray-
als we may sometimes witness due to human frailty
and sin.*

4. We read in n. 773: "Mary goes before us all in the holiness that is the Church's mystery as 'the bride without spot or wrinkle.' This is why the 'Marian' dimension of the Church precedes the 'Petrine' [the dimension represented by Peter and his successors, the Popes]."

What do you think this means?

*The Marian dimension stands for complete grace-filled responsiveness to Christ, which is another way of saying "holiness." The Petrine dimension is the authoritative, governing dimension represented especially by Peter and his successors, the Popes. To say that the Marian dimension **precedes** the Petrine dimension is to say that authority in the Church must always be **at the service of holiness.** Thus holy receptivity to the grace of God has "precedence." Of course this can never mean that one may invoke the Marian dimension in order to **disobey** Petrine authority and governance. This would be to divide the Body of Christ, to set it against itself, and that is in no way Marian or holy.*

5. The Catechism lists a number of characteristics of the People of God in n. 782. Discuss one or two that particularly struck you.

6. Read 1 Corinthians 12:27-31 and 13:1-13 on the various gifts or charisms God has bestowed on his people.

   - Do you think our culture is open to Paul's message that God has given different gifts to different people, that we can't simply choose the gift we want? Discuss.

   - Why do we, along with the Corinthians to whom Paul was writing, have such a need to hear the message of chapter 13 in light of the more "spectacular" gifts of prophecy, tongues, etc.?

7. We read in n. 791 that the unity of Christ's Body, the Church, "produces and stimulates charity among the faithful." Can you think of some evidence of this, both historically and in more recent times?

Consider that the works of mercy are a profound fruit of Christianity, which sees Christ in the least of our brethren (see Mt 25). Compassion for the sick and the dying, which led Christians to become the foremost builders of hospitals, beginning in the 4th century, is a classic trait of the followers of Christ. A typical example is St. Jerome Emiliani (1481-1537), whose compassion moved him to found not only a hospital, but orphanages and a shelter for women escaping prostitution. The same impulse of compassion can be seen over and over again, in St. Vincent de Paul, St. Margaret of Cortona, St. Elizabeth Ann Seton, St. Damien the Leper, Blessed Pier Giorgo Frassati, Blessed Mother Teresa of Calcutta, Dorothy Day. The number of men and women moved by the love of Christ to exceptional compassion for their brothers and sisters is practically endless. No doubt, everyone has seen examples of this in their own communities.

8. Conclude by having someone read aloud the quotes in small print in n. 795.

Session 5

One, Holy, Catholic and Apostolic

Reflection on
nn. 811-870

We reflect on the classic "four marks" that profoundly characterize the life of the Church and witness to the world her authenticity.

Discussion Questions

1. The Catechism notes that while the Church is "One," she is wounded in her unity by the various separations that have occurred in history. How would the Catechism have us think of, and relate to, the man or woman next door who is Lutheran or Episcopalian, etc. (See nn. 818, 819)?

*We recognize that their ecclesial community has many elements of truth and sanctification (Baptism, Scripture, etc.), and that it can even be a "means of salvation" for them. But if we accept that the Catholic Church has the **fullness** of truth and sanctification —offering the surest path to salvation—then we will look, in a discrete and sensitive way, for opportunities to share that fullness with our Protestant brethren, knowing that it will be of benefit to them and to the whole Body of Christ, and that it will correspond to the prayer of Jesus, "that they all may be one" (Jn 17:21).*

2. Have you ever been present at an ecumenical prayer service? If so, what was that experience like for you? What do you think is the value the Church sees in such initiatives?

3. How would you explain, to a non-Catholic, what we mean when we say that the Church is "Holy"? (see nn. 823-829).

*The Church's holiness is "real but imperfect" (n. 825) and it comes to her from the perfect holiness of Christ her Bridegroom. It is because she is his bride that she shares in his holiness, even though all of her **members** on earth (even her shepherds and saints—except the sinless Virgin Mary) must acknowledge that they are sinners. Thus we can say without contradiction that the Church is "at once holy and always in need of purification" (n. 827).*

4. The Catechism refers to the saints as models of holiness for the Church (n. 828). A great moral theologian once said the Faith of the Church is like a musical score or composition, and each saint is a beautifully *unique* rendition or performance of that score. What truth was he capturing? What stereotype of Christians does this insight help to combat?

There is a dual insight contained in this statement. On the one hand the Church's Faith is stable and constant, but on the other hand the saints are beautifully unique in the ways they live it out. Christians are not identical, "boring" paper cut-outs, as the worldly stereotype might suggest. A St. Francis of Assisi has his particular temperament and spirituality, different from a St. Ignatius of Loyola or a St. Teresa of Avila. But they are all faithful to the "musical score" of the Gospel, of the Church's Faith and teachings. The community of saints is like a beautiful garden in which delightful varieties of flowers flourish and give glory to God.

5. When we say that the Catholic Church is universal, in the sense that Christ wishes all men and women to belong to it, this strikes some people as proud or arrogant. Does it seem so to you? How can we profess it in a way that is actually quite humble—the very opposite of arrogance?

We simply acknowledge that the Church is not some proud creation of our own, but rather God's gift to us. We are humble, undeserving recipients of that gift, and we seek to follow Christ's command to "go and make disciples of all nations" (Mt 28:19), not because we are proud masters, but rather because we are humble servants of the Lord.

6. "Map out" the various levels of incorporation in the Catholic Church according to the Catechism in nn. 836-844. Is a baptized member of the Catholic Church always in the best position, the best relation to God (see n.837)?

Fully incorporated are faithful Catholics; then come members of the Orthodox Churches (who are very close to us in belief and who enjoy a valid priesthood and the seven sacraments); then other non-Catholic Christians ("ecclesial communities"); then the people of the Jewish faith, with whom we are especially linked by virtue of the Old Covenant; then Muslims, who profess faith in the One God, the God of Abraham; then, finally, all those religions that profess some belief in God.

We should note that ALL mankind is "ordered to" the Catholic Church (see n. 836). This expression means that God has designed us with the disposition and purpose of belonging to Christ's Body, the Church—just as a shovel is built to dig, or a pen to write.

This is true to such a degree that even those who do not know God in an explicit way may be incorporated in Christ's Body, the Church, if they seek to live in correspondence with the law God has written in their consciences (even without clear knowledge of the divine author of that law).

As to the second question, a baptized member of the Catholic Church is not always in the best position, the best relation to God. As we read in n. 837, "Even though incorporated into the Church, one who does not however persevere in charity is not saved. He remains indeed in the bosom of the Church, but 'in body' not 'in heart'" (Lumen Gentium, *14).*

So, for example, a primitive tribesman who knows nothing of Christ and the Gospel, but who is living according to the law that God has written in his heart and practicing love of neighbor, is clearly in a better position than a Catholic who does not persevere in charity. Of course, that same tribesman would be in a far richer and more secure relation with God, and have the advantage of many more graces and other helps (such as the Liturgy, Sacred Scripture and Church teaching) if he or she were baptized and professed the Catholic Faith.

7. Have you been in the position of evangelizing on behalf of the Catholic Church, or at least defending her from attack or misunderstanding? If so, what was that like for you? Do you think of yourself as an "apostle," as having an apostolate or mission? Discuss.

8. We read in n. 864 that "the fruitfulness of apostolate for ordained ministers as well as for lay people
   clearly depends on their vital union with Christ."
   What do you think is entailed in a "personal relationship with Jesus," and how do you think it
   changes a person's life and goals and relationships?

9. Conclude by having someone read the quote of St. Thérèse of Lisieux found in n. 826. Discuss what strikes you about it.

Session 6

One Body, Many Members

Reflection on
nn. 871-945

We now reflect on the many members in the one Body of Christ, the Church—hierarchy, laity and those in consecrated life.

Discussion Questions

1. In n. 875 we read that those in authority in the
    Church (the bishops) speak in the name of Christ
    and act by virtue of his authority. And yet in n. 876
    we read that they are to "become the slaves of all."
    How can this keep from being arrogant on the one
    hand, or soft and weak on the other?

    *It is not for their own power or glory that they speak
    in the name of Christ, for they can do so only be-
    cause he has given them the authority as his ambas-
    sadors. They have a responsibility to be faithful to
    that gift and mission given by Christ. Gratitude for
    the gift is appropriate, leading to dedication, but
    never to arrogance.*

    *As far as the risk of being soft or weak is concerned,
    they are not slaves in the sense that they are meant
    to be dominated by the laity or the world. Rather,
    their whole lives are meant to be put at the service of
    bringing Christ to their flock. This is loving, but it is
    certainly not "soft." Indeed, they are called to carry
    out their mission in strength and confidence, even
    confrontation where necessary, but always as ser-
    vants of their people's need to receive Christ and his
    Gospel into their hearts and souls.*

2. For many Catholics and others, the doctrine of infallibility (see nn. 889-891) is a stumbling block. Why? Imagine yourself called upon to present the best possible arguments in defense of infallibility. What would you say?

It is a stumbling block sometimes because people desire "wiggle room" to disobey something that they find challenging, and they think that teachings that are not infallible give them that. But here it is crucial to recall that even non-definitive Church teachings on faith and morals require the "religious assent of intellect and will," as noted in Lumen Gentium, *25, because even in her "ordinary" Magisterium (teachings), the Church is endowed with the authority of Christ and guided by the light of the Holy Spirit, and we are obliged to recognize that and to respond with trust and obedience.*

Other times people may reject the doctrine of infallibility because they misunderstand it, thinking that it means that literally everything the Pope says is infallible. But in fact the Pope exercises infallibility only when he "proclaims by a definitive act a doctrine pertaining to faith or morals" (LG, 25).

As support for the doctrine of infallibility, we can turn to various words of Christ: "You are Peter, and on this rock I will build my church, and the powers of death shall not prevail against it. I will give you the keys of the kingdom of heaven, and whatever you bind on earth shall be bound in heaven, and whatever you loose on earth shall be loosed in heaven" (Mt 16:18-19); "When the Spirit of truth comes, he will guide you into all the truth" (Jn 16:13); "He who hears you, hears me" (Lk 10:16); "Go therefore and make disciples of all nations...teaching them to observe all that I have commanded you; and lo, I am with you always, to the close of the age" (Mt 28:19-20).

Finally, one could argue that in granting the gift of infallibility, God recognizes that there are certain matters so central to the Faith that he wants us not only to give religious assent and obedience, but to have the absolute, unshakeable assurance of faith.

3. In n. 900, the Catechism says that the activity of the laity in Church communities "is so necessary that, for the most part, the apostolate of the pastors cannot be fully effective without it." What examples can you think of to show the truth of this statement?

4. Based on your reading of nn. 901-913, think care-
    fully about, and discuss, the various ways you as a
    lay person can be a *priest,* a *prophet* and a *king* in
    the image of Christ.

5. What is the difference between diocesan priests and priests who belong to religious orders, like the Jesuits or the Dominicans (see nn. 925-927)?

A diocesan priest is attached to a particular diocese and makes promises of celibacy and obedience to his bishop. He is typically assigned to minister in a parish. He does not make a promise of poverty, and usually owns a car and other possessions in order to live and carry out his ministry. A large majority of priests worldwide are diocesan.

A religious priest makes solemn vows of chastity, poverty and obedience. He belongs to a specific community that shares a common mission or charism (the charism of Dominicans, for example, is teaching). Each religious community has a rule of life and its members are subject to the direction of the superiors of their community. Religious priests typically do not oversee parishes, unless invited by the bishop of the diocese to do so and granted permission by their religious community.

6. In what way is someone who foregoes marriage to consecrate himself/herself to Christ a sign of the Kingdom to come (see nn. 916, 923, and 933)? Discuss the value and importance of this sign, perhaps especially in today's culture.

In heaven there will be no marrying or giving in marriage, so those in the consecrated life witness already to that reality. They are joined entirely to Christ, as will be the case in the Kingdom of Heaven, where the Church, the Bride of Christ, will be made entirely one with her Bridegroom. Also, they witness to freedom from the attachments of this world.

7. Have someone read n. 932.

    *   When you think of religious life in this profound and beautiful way, does some past or present example of religious life stand out in your mind?

    *   Have you personally encountered one or more examples of religious life or communities (teachers at a Catholic college or other institution, for example)?

    *   If so, try to relate your experience to what you have read of the consecrated life in the Catechism.

Session 7

Communion of Saints, Forgiveness of Sins

We now reflect on our belief in "the commu-nion of saints" and "the forgiveness of sins."

Discussion Questions

1. Besides discussing the communion of saints in the usual sense of a communion of *persons*, the Catechism talks about a communion of *holy things*. In n. 949, we read that one of these holy things is the faith itself, and that "faith is a treasure of life which is enriched by being shared." In what ways have you found your faith enriched through sharing it in this small group study?

2. In speaking of the communion of saints as an interconnection of persons in Christ, n. 953 states: "In this solidarity with all men, living or dead... the least of our acts done in charity redounds to the profit of all. Every sin harms this communion."

    - How would you creatively articulate and explain this to a child, a young person?
    - Are there any analogies that might be helpful?
    - How would you overcome the objection that some good and evil actions are "private," that they don't affect anybody else?

You could use the analogy of ecology. We may not realize it at first, but there is interdependence in the natural world that becomes evident when we begin misusing nature. For example, if we use certain toxic weed-killers in our yards (seemingly a "private" decision), eventually this runs off into our rivers and lakes and underground water sources, harming fish and wildlife and—most of all—ourselves and our neighbors. Our sins are like that, because we are all interconnected in the Body of Christ, forming a kind of spiritual "ecosystem." There is no such thing as a purely "private" choice. Staying with the same analogy in a positive direction, just as good stewardship of the created world and its resources benefits everyone, so, too, every act of love enriches the whole Body of Christ.

3. With regard to the communion of saints, read the quotes in small print from St. Dominic and St. Thérèse of Lisieux in n. 956.

    - How real to you does the presence of the saints seem? Discuss.
    - If we can go directly to Jesus in prayer (and of course we can), why do you suppose God, through his Church, encourages us to pray to the saints, asking their intercession?"

*If we can go directly to Jesus, why pray to the saints? Because God has made us a family in Christ, and he delights in our love and care for one another. That love and care does not end with death, but continues in the relations between heaven and earth (and purgatory). The saints are our older brothers and sisters, and God wills that they have a special role of intercession in our lives. He is not **jealous** of that relationship—it was his idea. It does nothing to detract from his own power and authority—indeed, it enhances it.*

4. Some people gravitate easily to devotion to the
    Blessed Virgin Mary. Others have to make more of
    a conscious effort to develop this.

    - What factors might contribute to these differ-
      ences?
    - What place has devotion to Mary had in your
      life, and what factors have shaped it one way
      or another? Are you satisfied or do you have
      further aspirations in this regard?
    - If you have a favorite prayer or devotion to
      Mary (or a favorite kind of picture or statue),
      reflect on why it is especially meaningful
      to you and share your reflections with the
      group.

*With regard to the ease with which one gravitates
to devotion to Mary, this may depend on how and
when the Blessed Virgin was introduced to us in our
religious formation, on whether our parents were
warmly devoted to her, on the kind of images, stat-
ues, and devotions we have been exposed to. These
are just some of many possible factors.*

5. As you reflect on nn. 964-972 on the role of the Virgin Mary, what especially stands out for you, and why? Critics of the Catholic Faith often charge that we "worship" Mary as a kind of goddess. What can we point to especially in nn. 970 and 971 to show that this is not the case?

See the indicated text.

6. In speaking of the Sacrament of Penance, n. 982 states: "There is no offense, however serious, that the Church cannot forgive." And yet Jesus says in Mark 3:29: "Whoever blasphemes against the Holy Spirit will never have forgiveness, but is guilty of an everlasting sin." How do you suppose we can possibly reconcile these apparently contradictory statements? (For help, look ahead to n. 1864 in the section on "Life in Christ.")

The Catechism indicates in n. 1864 that the sin against the Holy Spirit is the sin of hardness of heart in which a person obstinately refuses to repent. So it is not a matter of a specific offense that is un-forgivable, but rather the refusal to express sorrow for sin and to ask God's pardon. Like the father in the Parable of the Prodigal Son, God is always eager to forgive and to show mercy, but he will not force it on a sinner who is unwilling to repent.

Session 8

Resurrection of the Body and Life Everlasting

Reflection on nn. 988-1065

We conclude our study of the Creed by reflecting on our belief in "the resurrection of the body" and "life everlasting."

Discussion Questions

1. As noted in n. 994, Jesus gave us a sign of the future resurrection in his restoring some of the dead to life (e.g., Lazarus). Jesus' own Resurrection was the most powerful sign of all, and "of another order" than these other restorations of life. In what way was his Resurrection different from the raising of Lazarus?

Lazarus was restored to mortal, earthly life, but he would die again. Jesus rose to a glorified life, the same glorified life he will allow the saved to share when he raises them on the last day, never to die again. Jesus' glorified body has new and mysterious properties. He is able to appear and disappear at will, to veil his identity—for example, from Mary Magdelene by the tomb (Jn 20:11-15), and from the disciples on the road to Emmaus (Lk 24:15-16). This risen, glorified form of existence is beyond our comprehension, surpassing mortal, earthly life.

2. With regard to the implications of our future resurrection, n. 1004 quotes St. Paul's words: "The body
    [is meant] for the Lord, and the Lord for the body.
    And God raised the Lord and will also raise us up
    by his power. Do you not know that your bodies are
    members of Christ? ...You are not your own; ...So
    glorify God in your body" (1 Cor 6:13-15, 19-20). If
    everyone in our world really believed this and embraced it, what differences would we see in people's
    lives and in the culture as a whole?

3. According to the Catechism, death is simultane-
    ously the bitter consequence of sin and the sweet
    path to eternal life in Christ. It follows that there is
    something of darkness and pain, yet something of
    light and hope, in death, from a Christian perspec-
    tive. What experiences of death have you had, in
    relation to family, friends, etc.? Share whatever you
    wish regarding the way death has touched you.

4. In n. 1007 the point is made that "remembering our mortality helps us realize that we have only a limited time in which to bring our lives to fulfill-ment." If you flash forward in your imagination to that moment when it will be *you* lying in the coffin at the foot of the altar, with mourners all around, what impact does that have on how you want to live your life in the present? What becomes important? What becomes less significant? Read the quotes in fine print in n. 1014 and 1039.

5. The Catechism notes that in the litany of the saints we pray: "From a sudden and unforeseen death, deliver us, O Lord." Other quotes in n. 1014 echo this theme. Yet many people say that when it is time for them to die they would like to go very quickly. Some even say they would prefer to die suddenly in their sleep. Why do you suppose this attitude is so common today, and the Church's approach relatively rare?

It is often motivated by the fear of a lingering, painful, humiliating death. This is very human and understandable. But it may also be motivated by an unfortunate lack of concern for one's soul and for the precious opportunity provided by a period of prayer and of reconciliation with God and neighbor before one's entrance into the next life. Perhaps it reflects a certain presumption that God will find me to be "just fine the way I am" when I stand before him.

6. Of heaven, Scripture says, "No eye has seen, nor ear heard, nor the heart of man conceived, what God has prepared for those who love him" (1 Cor. 2:9). Read also the Catechism's quote of St. Cyprian in fine print in n. 1028. The saints often have *longed* to die so they could be with God in heaven (see nn. 1010 and 1011). Most of us, on the other hand, cling tenaciously to earthly life. What accounts for the difference, in your estimation?

7. Some people imagine purgatory to be a kind of "mini-hell," where God inflicts mere punishment on people for their sins which haven't been completely expiated on earth. How would you correct that point of view, drawing on insights from the Catechism (see nn. 1030, 1031)?

*The purification of the elect is "entirely different from the punishment of the damned" (1031), for those in purgatory die in God's friendship. We do not know the exact nature of their purification, but we can imagine that they **desire** to undergo it because they wish to be completely clean when they stand before their Lord and their God.*

8. Of hell, the Catechism states: "Immediately after death the souls of those who die in a state of mortal sin descend into hell, where they suffer the punishments of hell, 'eternal fire.' The chief punishment of hell is eternal separation from God...." (n. 1035). How would you defend this teaching against the objection of someone who argued that a loving God would never condemn anyone to such a place as hell?

*We read in n. 1037: "God predestines no one to go to hell; for this, a willful turning away from God (a mortal sin) is necessary, and **persistence in it until the end**" (emphasis added). It is a "self-exclusion from communion with God and the blessed" (1033). Finally, as n. 1034 and the passages cited in footnote 612 amply attest, the doctrine on hell is not the invention of the Catholic Church, but a reality firmly taught by Christ himself in the Gospels. The reality of hell shows God's supreme respect for human freedom.*

9. Based on nn.1042-1050, summarize what we know about the "New Heaven and New Earth" to come. What does the Catechism acknowledge we do *not* know?

We know:

- *The Church will receive her perfection;*

- *The human race will be one in Christ;*

- *The visible universe will be transformed, restored to its original state, sharing the glorification of the just in the risen Christ;*

- *The fruits of our work on earth will be found again, cleansed and transfigured.*

We do not know "the moment of the consummation of the earth and of man, nor the way in which the universe will be transformed" (n. 1048).

10. This session concludes your study of the Creed, which constitutes, it is fair to say, the cornerstone of the *Catechism of the Catholic Church*. You should be congratulated, for you have made your way through 1065 paragraphs filled with significance and beauty, roughly 275 pages! What do you hope will be a fruit of this study in your life?

The Discipleship Series

Novo Millennio Press